AF255641

# Manuel McFeely

# GET STARTED PROGRAMMING WITH PYTHON

*Give your professional possibilities a boost by learning the Python programming language*

# TABLE OF CONTENTS

# INTRODUCTION

Python is a fantastic programming language to learn, and it can be applied to a wide range of software development projects. Python can be used for a variety of tasks, including web development, data analysis, machine learning, and artificial intelligence.

Guido Rossum designed Python in 1989 as an object-oriented programming language. It's perfect for rapid prototyping complicated applications. It may be extended to C or C++ and has interfaces to numerous OS system calls and libraries. Python is used by many significant corporations, including NASA, Google, YouTube, BitTorrent, and others.

Python is intended to be a very understandable language. It typically uses English terms instead of punctuation, and it has fewer syntactical structures than other languages.

Python is a must-have skill for students and working professionals who want to become exceptional software engineers, especially if they work in the Web Development field.

You'll study the fundamentals of the Python programming language in this course, and you'll learn how to utilize Python.

You will also find many helpful but straightforward exercises to immediately practice what you have learned, assimilate the notions, and make them your own in the long run. What you'll learn, you will never forget!

So, what do you say, shall we start?

# Chapter 1. INSTALLING PYTHON

The first step in becoming a Python coder is to install or update Python on your computer. You may install Python using a package manager, obtain official Python distributions from Python.org, or install customized distributions for scientific computing, IoT, and embedded devices.

This tutorial focuses on official releases because they're the greatest way to get started learning Python programming.

You will learn how to:

- Check the Python version that is installed on your computer if any;
- Update or Install Python on Windows, macOS, and Linux; and
- Use Python on mobile devices such as phones and tablets
- Use online interpreters to use Python on the web.

This book will help you no matter what operating system you're using. Choose your operating system from the list below and get started!

# INSTALLING PYTHON ON WINDOWS

On Windows, there are three installation options:

1. The Microsoft Store
2. The full installer
3. Linux Subsystem for Windows

In this chapter, you will learn how to check which version of Python is installed on your Windows machine. You'll also discover which of the three installation options is best for you.


## How to find out what python version you have on windows

Open a command-line application, such as PowerShell to see if Python is already installed on your Windows PC.

Here's how to start PowerShell:

1. Press the Win key on your keyboard.
2. Type PowerShell into the search box.
3. Hit the Enter key.

You may also right-click the Start button and choose Windows PowerShell or Windows PowerShell for PowerShell (Admin).

You can also use Windows Terminal or cmd.exe.

Insert this command into the command prompt and click Enter:

```
C:\> python –version
Python 3.8.4
```

You can find out what version is installed by using the —version switch. You can also use the -V switch to achieve the same result:

```
C:\> python –V
Python 3.8.4
```

In either case, you'll want to upgrade your installation if it's older than 3.8.4, and it was the most recent version at the time of writing.

Note: If you don't have a Python version installed, each of the following statements will open the Microsoft Store and take you to the Python program page. In the next section, you'll learn how to finish the installation through the Microsoft Store.

You can use the where.exe command in cmd.exe or PowerShell to find out where the installation is located:

- C:\> where.exe python
- C:\Users\mertz\AppData\Local\Programs\Python\Python37-32\python.exe

It's worth noting that the where.exe command will only work if your user account has Python installed.

What are your choices? Are

There are several ways to install the official Python distribution on Windows, as previously mentioned:

1. Microsoft Store package: On Windows, the most basic installation is to use the Microsoft Store program. Beginner Python users searching for an easy-to-set-up interactive experience should try this.
2. Full Installer: This technique entails downloading Python from the Python.org website directly. Intermediate and advanced developers that require additional control over the setup process should use this.
3. Windows Subsystem for Linux (WSL): The WSL enables you to operate a Linux environment in a Windows environment.

Only the first two alternatives, which are the most common installation techniques in a Windows system, will be covered in this section.

If you want to install under the WSL, go straight to the Linux section of this article after you've installed your preferred Linux distribution.

Note: Alternative distributions, such as Anaconda, can be used to complete the installation on Windows; however, this article only covers official distributions.

Anaconda is a well-known Python environment for scientific computing and data science.

There are differences between the two official Python installers for Windows. There are some significant limits to the Microsoft Store bundle.

The Microsoft Store Package's Limitations

The Microsoft Store package is described as follows in the official Python documentation:

The Microsoft Store package is a user-friendly Python interpreter designed primarily for interactive use, such as by students.

The most important point is that the Microsoft Store bundle is "primarily designed for interactive use." That is to say, the Microsoft Store package is intended for students and people who are learning Python for the first time.

The Microsoft Store package has constraints that make it unsuitable for a professional development environment and aimed towards novice Pythonistas. It doesn't have full write access to shared folders like TEMP or the registry, for example.

## Recommendations from the windows installer

Install from Microsoft Store if you are new to Python and want to study the language rather than build professional software. This is the easiest and quickest way to get started with the least amount of hassle.

The official Python.org installation, on the other hand, is the ideal choice if you're an experienced developer wishing to develop professional software in a Windows environment. Microsoft Store regulations won't restrict you, and you'll be able to choose where the executable is installed, as well as add Python to your PATH if necessary.

## How to get it from microsoft's store

If you're new to Python and want to get started quickly, the Microsoft Store package is the most convenient technique to get started. Two steps are required to install through the Microsoft Store.

Step 1: In the Microsoft Store, go to the Python App Page.

Search for Python on the Microsoft Store app.

You'll probably notice a few different versions to choose from:

To launch the installation screen, select Python 3.8 or the highest version number available in the app.

Warning: Double-check that the Python program you've chosen is from the Python Software Foundation.

The official Microsoft Store bundle will always be free; therefore, it's not the right software if an app costs money.

You can also launch PowerShell and enter the following command:

```
C:\> python
```

If you don't already have a version of Python installed, pressing Enter will activate the Microsoft Store, which will take you to the most recent version of Python available.

Step 2: Download and install the Python application.

After you've decided which version to install, continue the installation by following these steps:

1. Click Get.
2. Wait for the application to complete the download process. The Get button will be replaced by an Install on my devices button when the download is complete.

3. Select the devices on which you would like to complete the installation by clicking Install on my devices.

4. To begin the installation, click Install Now and then OK.

5. If the installation went smoothly, the notification "This product is installed" will appear at the top of the Microsoft Store page.

Congratulations! Python, including pip and IDLE, is now available to you!


## How to install from the full installer

Installing via the complete installer is the best option for expert developers that require a full-featured Python programming environment. Installing via the Microsoft Store provides less customization and control over the installation.

In two steps, you can install from the full installer.

Step 1: Download the Full Installer

To get the full installer, follow these steps:

1. Go to the Python.org

2. Click link for the Latest Python 3 Release - Python 3. x.x under the headline "Python

Releases for Windows." Python 3.8.4 was the most recent version at the time of writing.

3. Navigate to the bottom of the page and choose either the 64-bit Windows x86-64 executable installer or the 32-bit Windows x86 executable installer.

If you are unsure whether to use the 32-bit or 64-bit installation, expand the box below for more information.

32-bit or 64-bit Python?

Show/Hide

Move to the next step once the installer has finished downloading.

Step 2: Launch the Setup Program

After you have selected and downloaded an installer, double-click on it to launch it. A dialog window will pop up, similar to the one below:

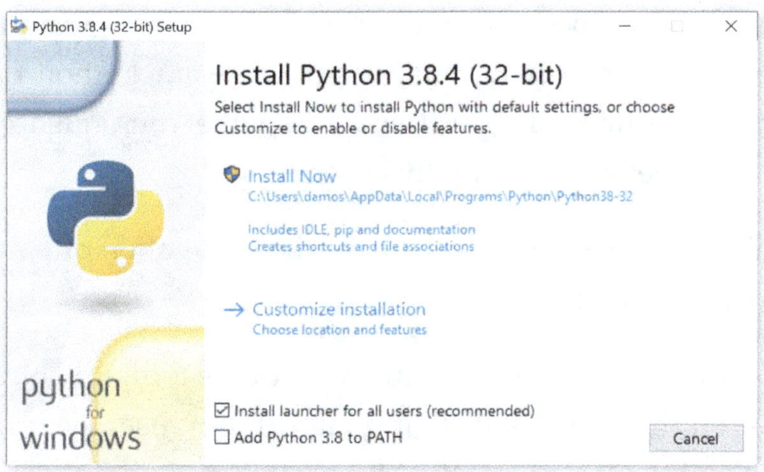


There are 4 things to keep in mind when looking at this dialog box:

1. The default install path is in the current Windows user's AppData/ directory.
2. The Specify installation button allows you to customize the installation location and which additional features, such as pip and IDLE, are installed.
3. By default, the Install app for all users (recommended) checkbox is enabled. This means that the py.exe launcher will be

accessible to all users on the machine. This box can be unchecked to limit Python to the current Windows user.

4.  By default, the Add Python 3.8 to PATH checkbox is unchecked. There are various reasons why you would not want Python on your PATH, so think about the consequences before checking this option.

You have absolute control over the installation process with the full installer.

Warning: If you are unfamiliar with the term PATH, it is strongly advised that you do not use the full installer. Instead, get the Microsoft Store bundle.

Use the settings on the dialog box to customize the installation to match your needs. Then press the Install Now button. It's as simple as that!

You now have the latest version of Python 3 installed on your Windows PC!

# HOW TO SETUP PYTHON ON A MAC

On previous versions of macOS, Python 2 comes preloaded. Starting with macOS Catalina, this is no longer the case for current versions of macOS.

On macOS, there are two installation options:

1. The formal installation program
2. The package manager for Homebrew

This chapter will teach you how to determine which version of Python is installed on your Mac. You'll also discover which of the two installation procedures is best for you.

## On a mac, how can you check your python version?

Open a command-line application, such as Terminal, to see the Python version you have on your Mac.

Here's how to start Terminal:

1. Press the Cmd+Space keys at the same time.
2. Select a terminal.
3. Hit the Enter key.

You can also open Finder and go to Applications Utilities Terminal.

Type the following commands into the command prompt:

- # Check the system Python version

  $ python --version
- # Check the Python 2 version

  $ python2 --version
- # Check the Python 3 version

  $ python3 --version

If your machine has Python installed, one or more of these tasks should return a version number.

If Python 3.6.10 was already installed on your computer, the python3 program would show the following version number:

- $ python3 –version

  Python 3.6.10

If any of the following circumstances apply to you, you should download the most recent version of Python:

- None of the commands listed above return a version number.
- The Python 2. X series is the only version that appears.
- You don't have the most recent version of Python 3, version 3.8.4, as of this writing.

What are your choices?

On macOS, there are two options for installing the official Python distribution:

1.  The official installer is as follows: This technique entails downloading and installing the official Python installer from the Python.org website.
2.  The package manager for homebrew: If you don't already have it installed, you'll need to download and install the Homebrew package manager and then type a command into a terminal application.

The Homebrew package manager and official installer will function, although the Python Software Foundation exclusively maintains the official installation.

Note: Alternative distributions, such as Anaconda, can be used to complete the installation on macOS; however, this book only covers official distributions.

Anaconda is a well-known Python environment for scientific computing and data science. Check out the official Anaconda documentation's macOS installation instructions to discover how to install Anaconda on your Mac.

The Homebrew package manager and The official installer both install different distributions. There are various drawbacks to installing from Homebrew.

Installing Homebrew Has Its Limits

The Tcl/Tk requirement required by the Tkinter module is not included in the Python installation for macOS available on Homebrew. Tkinter is a Python library module for creating graphical user interfaces. It is an interface for the Tk GUI toolkit, which isn't included in Python.

Homebrew does not install the Tk GUI toolkit required. Instead, it uses a version that is already installed on your system. You may be unable to import the Tkinter module because the system version of Tcl/Tk is old or missing entirely.

## Macos installer recommendations

Because it's easy to administer from the command line and allows commands to update Python without going to a website, the Homebrew package manager is a popular option for installing Python on macOS. Because Homebrew is a command-line program, bash scripts can be used to automate it.

The Python distribution provided by Homebrew, on the other hand, is not under the control of the Python

Software Foundation and may change at any time. The official installer is the most dependable approach on macOS, especially if you plan on performing Python GUI programming with Tkinter.

## How to use the official installer to install

On macOS, installing Python through the official installer is the most trustworthy option. It contains all of the system dependencies required for Python application development.

In two steps, you can install via the official installer.

Step 1: Download the Official Installer

To get the full installer, follow these steps:

1. Go to the Python.org
2. Click the link for the Latest Python
3. To begin the download, scroll to the bottom and click macOS 64-bit installer.

Proceed to the next step once the installer has finished downloading.

Step 2: Launch the Setup Program

launch the installer. The following window should appear:

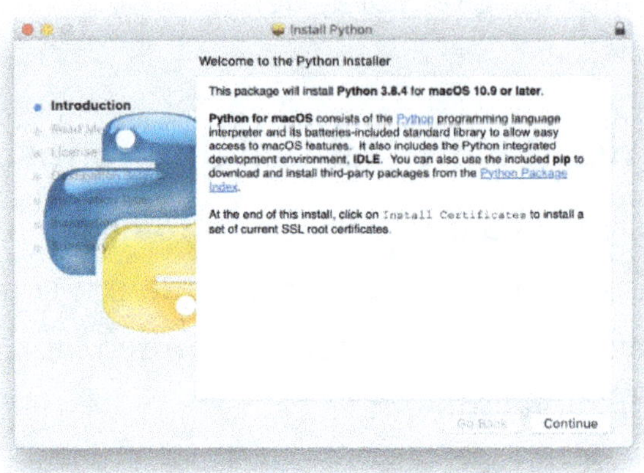

To finish the installation, follow these steps:

1. Keep pressing Continue until you're prompted to accept the software license agreement. After that, click Agree.

2. You'll see a window that tells you where the installation will take place and how much space it will need. You're probably not going to modify the default location, so click Install to begin the installation.

3. When the installer has finished copying files, close the installation window by clicking Close.

You now have the most recent version of Python 3 installed on your Mac!

# Installing from homebrew

The Homebrew package management is a viable alternative for people who need to install from the command line, especially if they won't utilize Python to construct graphical user interfaces with the Tkinter module. In two steps, you may install via the Homebrew package manager.

Step 1: Install Homebrew

You can skip this step if you already have Homebrew installed. If you don't already have Homebrew installed, follow the steps below to do so:

1. Launch your browser and go to http://brew.sh/.
2. Near the top of the page, under the title "Install Homebrew," you should notice command for installing Homebrew. This command will look something like this:
3. $ /bin/bash -c "$(curl -fsSL https://raw.githubusercontent.com/Homebrew/install/master/install.sh)" To copy the command to your clipboard, select it with your cursor and hit Cmd+C.
4. Paste the command into a terminal window and hit Enter. This will start the installation of Homebrew.

5. When prompted, type your macOS user password.

   Depending on your Internet connection, it may take several minutes to download all of Homebrew's essential files. You'll be back at the shell prompt in your terminal window once the installation is finished.

Note: If you're using macOS for the first time, you could encounter a pop-up requesting you install Apple's command line developer tools. Because these tools are required for installation, click Install to approve the dialog box.

You'll need to click Enter to continue installing Homebrew after the development tools have been installed.

You're ready to install Python now that Homebrew is installed.

Step 2: Install Python

To finish the Homebrew installation, follow these steps:

1. Launch a terminal program.
2. To upgrade Homebrew, do the following command:

3.  Brew update && brew upgrade ($ brew update
    && brew upgrade)

Installing Python 3 with Homebrew is now as simple as typing brew install python3. This will install the most current version of Python on your computer.

Check if you can access Python from the terminal to ensure everything went smoothly:

1.  To begin, open a terminal.
2.  Press Enter after typing pip3.
3.  The help text from Python's pip package management should appear. If you receive an error message when executing pip3, repeat the installation procedures to successful installation.

Congratulations, Python is now installed on your Mac!

# PYTHON FEATURES

We had about as many programming languages at some point in time as we could count on our fingertips. There are so many here today, and all with their specialties. What makes a language unique, however, are its features. And in the end, it's its features that make it selected or passed for a project. So, before we start with deeper Python concepts, let's first look at the basics of Python's programming language, which justifies the reasons behind what makes Python so powerful compared to other programming languages. So, let's start with the Python Programing Language Features.

## Python Features

### 1. Easy

We mean it in different contexts when we say the word 'easy.'

### a. Simple to code

Python is very easy to code as we have seen in earlier lessons. Coding in Python is easier compared with other common languages such as C++ and Java. In just a few hours anyone can learn the Python syntax.

Mastering Python, though sure, requires learning about all of its advanced concepts and packages and modules. It takes time. And it's programmer-friendly.

## b. Simple to Read

Python programming is somewhat like English, being a high-level language. If you look at it, you can tell what the code should be doing. It also requires indentation, since it is dynamically-typed. This helps in readability.

## 2. Expressive

Let's first learn on expressiveness. Assume we have two languages A and B, and the local transformations can be used to make all programs that can be made in A. There are however some programs that can be made using local transformations in B, but not in A. Then, it says B is more expressive than A. Python offers us a multitude of constructs that help us focus more on the solution than on the syntax. This is one of the outstanding features of python which tells you why you should learn Python.

## 3. Free & Open Source

Firstly, Python is available freely. This can be downloaded from the Python Website.

Second, they are open-source. That means the public has access to its source code. You can download them, change them, use them and distribute them. This is called FLOSS(Free / Free Software and Open Source). As the Python community, we 're all headed towards one goal — a Python that's getting even better.

## 4. High-Level

As we discussed in point 2b, this is a vocabulary of high quality. This means we do not need to remember the system architecture as programmers. We needn't control the memory either. That makes it more programmer-friendly and is one of the key features of python.

## 5. Portable

Let's say you wrote a Python file for your Windows computer. But if you want to run it on a Pc, you don't have to make the same improvements to it. In other words, you can take 1 code and run it on any machine; for different machines, there is no need to write different code. This makes for a compact language for Python. In this case, however, you need to avoid any system-dependent features.

## 6. Interpreted Version

If you are familiar with any languages such as Java or C++, you need to compile it first, then run it. But it doesn't need to be compiled at Python. Internally, it transforms the source code into an immediate form, called bytecode. So, just running your Python code without thinking about connecting to libraries and a few other things is all you need to do.

By reading, we say that the source code is run line by line, and not all at once. Because of this, debugging the code is simpler. Interpreting also makes it slightly slower than Java, but that doesn't matter when compared with the advantages that it has to bring.

## 7. Goal-focused

It is said that it is an object-oriented programming language that can model the real world. It focuses on objects and puts together data and functions. Contrary to this, a language geared towards procedures revolves around functions, which are code that can be reused. Python supports both procedure-oriented programming and object-oriented programming which is one of the key features of python. In contrast to Java, it also supports multiple inheritances. A class is a blueprint for an object like this. It is an abstract type of data, and contains no values.

## 8. Enlarge

You may write some of your Python code in other languages such as C++, if necessary. This makes Python an extensible language, which means it can be extended to include other languages.

240 + Python Tutorials – Master Python programming in real-time and practical projects.

## 9. Embedded

We've just seen that we can insert code into our Python source code in other languages. However, you can also bring our Python code into a source code in another language like C++. This enables us to integrate the scripting capabilities into the other language program.

## 10. Large Standard Library

Python downloads that you can use with a large library so you don't have to write your code for every single thing. There are libraries for regular expressions, generation of documents, unit testing, web browsers, threading, databases, CGI, email, image manipulation, and many other features.

## 11. Programmable GUI

Until their GUI is made a software is not user-friendly. A user can interact easily with a GUI to the software. Python provides a range of libraries to render

Graphical UI for your applications. You may make use of Tkinter, wxPython, or JPython for this. These toolkits allow you to build GUI easily and quickly.

## 12. Typed Dynamically

Python is typed dynamically. This means that you decide the type for a value at runtime, not beforehand. Therefore, we do not need to specify the data type while declaring it.

The python programming language tutorial features are all about this.

# THE BENEFITS OF PYTHON LEARNING

There are many advantages of studying and working with Python.

For example, learning is extremely simple and can be used as a move in other languages and frameworks such as PERL, C, C++, and more. If you are an absolute beginner and this is your first time working with any kind of coding language, that is certainly something you want. Once you complete your training, you'll have plenty of opportunities to grow, if necessary, rather than being confined to one language.

Python is then popular because it is commonly used. So famous, that several tech giants like Instagram, Google, Pinterest, Yahoo use this! – IBM, Disney, Nokia, etc. Once you've learned Python, there'll never be a shortage of ways to use that skill. You can make good cash as a Python developer because a lot of big companies rely on the language.

**Many advantages include:**

1) Python can be used in product production and can help speed up the idea of the design process as it is so easy to use and to understand.

2) Python is ideally suited for general purpose tasks such as data mining and the facilitation of big data.

3) Developers of all ability levels prefer to remain more coordinated and efficient as compared to languages like C # and Java as operating with Python.

4) Python is easy to read, even if you are not an experienced programmer, so it is ideal for use among multi-programmers and large development teams, especially those with inexperienced coding team members.

5) Django is a comprehensive and open-source Web application framework powered by Python. Frameworks – like Ruby on Rails – simplify the process of development by allowing developers to work with existing code snippets called modules. These packets of code can be modified and repurposed over multiple projects as necessary.

6) Because Python is an open-source language and a developed community, it has a massive base of support. Millions of like-minded developers frequently interact with the language. Additionally, the community works together continuously to improve core functionality. This is also a perfect place for other developers to network.

# Chapter 2.   GETTING YOU STARTED WITH PYTHON PROGRAMMING

## STEP 1: DECIDE WHY YOU WANT TO LEARN PYTHON.

Evaluate why you want to learn Python in the first place before you start learning it online. This is because it will be a lengthy and, at times, unpleasant journey. If you don't have enough motivation, you won't make it. Finding out what motivates you can help you set a long-term goal and a path to get there without becoming bored. You do not need to develop a specific project to study Python, just a general area of interest.

Choose an area that interests you, such as:

- Data science / Machine learning
- Mobile apps
- Websites
- Games
- Data processing and analysis
- Hardware / Sensors / Robots

- Scripts to automate your work

# STEP 2: ACQUIRE A BASIC SYNTAX UNDERSTANDING

This stage, on the other hand, cannot be bypassed. You must first master the foundations of Python syntax before digging deeper into your chosen field. Because it isn't extremely inspiring, you should invest as little time possible on it.

I cannot emphasize enough the importance of spending as little time as possible on basic syntax. You will learn more quickly if you start working on things as soon as possible. If you get stuck later, you can always go back to the syntax. You should only spend a couple of weeks on this phase and no more than a month on it.

Also, a brief reminder: Python 3 is the version to learn, not Python 2. Unfortunately, many online "learn Python" sites still teach Python 2, while Python 3 is the way to go. Bugs and security flaws in Python 2 will not be patched because it is no longer supported!

# STEP 3: CREATE WELL-ORGANIZED PROJECTS

It's possible to start developing projects on your own once you've mastered the basic syntax. Projects are a terrific technique to learn since they allow you to put what you've learned into practice. It will be difficult to remember your information until you put it to use. Projects will help you stretch your strengths, gain new skills, and build a portfolio to present potential employers.

However, freeform projects will be painful at this point, as you'll get stuck frequently and need to consult the documentation. As a result, it's usually best to start with more structured tasks until you're confident enough to build projects entirely independently. Many learning resources provide structured projects, which allow you to create fascinating things in the areas that interest you while also preventing you from being stuck.

Let's have a look at some useful resources for structured initiatives in each of these areas:

**Machine learning / Data science**

- Python for Data Analysis is a decent introduction to analyzing data in Python,

published by the author of a prominent Python
  data analysis library.
- Dataquest - A fun way to learn Python and data
  science. You examine a wide range of datasets,
  including CIA documents and NBA player
  statistics. Finally, complex algorithms like
  neural networks and decision trees are created.
- Scikit-learn documentation — Scikit-learn is a
  popular Python machine learning package. It
  includes a wealth of documentation and
  lessons.
- CS109 is a Harvard course that teaches Python
  in a data science environment. Some of their
  work, as well as other materials, are accessible
  over the internet.

**Apps for mobile devices**

- Kivy tutorial — Kivy is a Python-based tool for
  creating mobile apps. They provide a step-by-
  step tutorial on how to get started.

**Websites**

- How To Tango With Django — An introduction
  to Django, a powerful Python web framework.
- Bottle tutorial - Another Python web framework
  is Bottle. This is where you should begin.

**Games**

- Pygame tutorials — This is a list of Pygame tutorials. Pygame is a popular Python package for developing games.
- Codecademy – guides you through the process of creating a couple of easy games.

- Pygame: Making Games — This book shows you how to make games in Python.
- Invent Your Videogames with Python — a book that shows you how to use Python to create a range of games.

A game was created with Pygame as an example. Phil Hassey created Barbie Seahorse Adventures 1.0.

Robots/Hardware/Sensors

- Using Arduino with Python — learn how to control sensors connected to an Arduino using Python.
- Build hardware projects with Python and a Raspberry Pi while learning Python.
- Python for Robotics – program robots using Python.
- Raspberry Pi Cookbook — learn how to use the Raspberry Pi and Python to make robots.

**Scripts to Make Your Work More Automated**

- Automate the mundane with Python – learn how to use Python to automate every daytasks.

You should work on your projects after completing a few organized assignments in your field. But, first and foremost, you should invest some time understanding how to solve difficulties.

# STEP 4: WORK ON YOUR PERSONAL PYTHON PROJECTS

It's time to work on your projects to expand your Python expertise after finishing numerous predefined tasks. You'll still use resources and understand concepts, and you'd be performing tasks that you're passionate about. Before you start working on your projects, you should be comfortable debugging errors and problems with your applications. The following materials should be familiar to you:

- StackOverflow – a question-and-answer platform where programmers can discuss their problems. Python-specific questions can be found here.
- Google — every experienced programmer's go-to search engine. When trying to fix problems, this tool comes in handy. Here's an illustration.
- Python documentation - a fantastic place to go for Python reference material.

Once you've mastered troubleshooting challenges, you can start working on your projects. It's a good idea to work on issues that you're interested in. For example, I started working on automated stock trading programs quickly after learning programming.

**Tips on how to locate interesting projects:**

- Add more features to the projects you were working on previously.
- Take a look at our beginning Python projects.
- Attend local Python gatherings to meet people who are working on interesting projects.
- search for open-source projects to make contribution to.
- Look into whether any local NGOs need volunteer developers.
- Look at projects that others have completed and see if you can expand or adapt them. Github is a great location to look for them.
- Look through other people's blog postings to get ideas for projects.
- Consider what tools would make your day-to-day life easier, and then create them.

Always remember to start small. To acquire confidence, it's often a good idea to start with something easy. It is preferable to start a small project and finish it than to start a large job and never finish it. We offer guided projects at Dataquest that give you tiny data science-related tasks on which you can build.

Finding other people to work with can also help you stay motivated.

If you're stuck for project ideas, here are a few in each of the areas we've covered:

**Machine Learning / Data Science Project Concepts**

- A map that depicts state-by-state election polling.
- An algorithm that forecasts your location's weather.
- A stock market forecasting program.
- An algorithm that summaries news stories automatically.

**Mobile App Project Ideas**

- An app that keeps track of how far you walk each day.
- An app that delivers you weather notifications.
- A location-based communication in real-time.

**Website Project Ideas**

- A website that assists you in planning your weekly meals.
- A website where people may rate and review video games.
- A platform for taking notes.

**Python Game Project Ideas**

- A mobile game in which you capture territory based on your location.
- A puzzle-solving game in which you program.

**Robots/Hardware/Sensors Project Concepts**

- Sensors that monitor your home's temperature and allow you to keep an eye on it from afar.
- A more intelligent alarm clock.
- An obstacle-detecting self-driving robot.

**Work Automation Project Ideas**

- A script to automate data entry
- A tool for extracting data from the internet.

My first solo effort was porting my R-based automated essay scoring program to Python. It didn't turn out to be particularly attractive, but it provided me a sense of success and set me on the path of improving my talents.

The secret is to pick a task and finish it. You might never finish a job if you get too caught up in choosing the right one.

# STEP 5: CONTINUE TO WORK ON MORE CHALLENGING PROJECTS.

Extend the scope and difficulty of your task to keep challenging yourself. It is time to try something new if you're completely content with what you've done.

You can start a new project if you want to.

**Here are some suggestions for when that moment arrives:**

- Teach a beginner how to develop a project you created.
- • Is it feasible to expand the scope of your tool? Is it able to process more information or handle more traffic?
- Is there a way to make your program run faster?
- Can you make your tool more valuable to a wider audience?
- How would you market what you've created?

**In the future**

Python is a dynamic language. Only a few people can claim to fully know the language, and they are the ones who created it.

You must continue to study and work on assignments at all times. You'll be looking back over your code from six months ago and thinking how horrible it is if you do it correctly.

Python is a very entertaining and gratifying language to learn, and I believe that anyone with the appropriate motivation can master it.

# CHOOSING A PROJECT PLATFORM

You need to develop your program to run on a platform, so you can use your program for people who lack other technical knowledge. The desktop, web, and command-line are the 3 major platforms for which you would like to build your projects.

## Website

Web applications are applications running on the web, they can be accessed without downloading on any device, providing access to the internet is available. If you want someone with internet access to access your projects it needs to be a web application.

A Web application has a front end and a back end. The back-end i where the business logic is: the data is manipulated and stored by your backend code. The front end is the application interface: your front-end code will determine what a web application looks like.

Your main focus as an intermediate Python developer will be on the back-end code. However, the front-end code is also essential so you'll need some CSS, HTML, and maybe JavaScript knowledge to construct a simple-looking GUI. Just the basics would suffice.

Another option is to use Python for the front end as well as back end. You can focus on Python code alone thanks to the anvil library which eliminates the need for HTML, JavaScript, and CSS.

With Python, you can create web applications through web frameworks such as Django and flask. The list of frameworks used to build web apps using Python is long. There's plenty to choose from but the most popular web frameworks remain Django and flask.

## Desktop Graphics

It is through an application whenever you perform a task on your PC, whether it's a desktop or laptop. You can also make your desktop applications as an intermediate Python developer.

As you've seen with web applications, you don't have to learn any front-end technology to create your Graphical User Interface ( GUI) applications. All the parts can be built using Python.

Frameworks exist to build your desktop applications. PySimpleGUI is one of them, and an intermediate Python developer finds it pretty user-friendly.

An advanced GUI framework such as PyQt5 is quite powerful, but perhaps it has a steep learning curve.

The Desktop GUI program you build will operate on all of the Windows, Linux, or Mac operating systems. After creating the project all you need to do is compile it to an executable for your preferred operating system.

## Control-Line

Command-line apps are those apps that work in a console window. This is the Windows command prompt, and the Linux and Mac Screen.

You would click to use a web or GUI application, but for command-line applications, you would type in commands. Command-line software users need to have some technical expertise, because they may need to use commands.

Command-line applications can not be as beautiful or as user-friendly as web or GUI applications, but this does not make them less effective than web or GUI.

By adding colors to the text, you can enhance the look of your Command-line applications. There are libraries that you can use to color, such as color and Colorama. You should spice up things and use a few colors.

You can build your applications using frameworks such as Docopt, Argparse, and click.

## Ideas for web project

You'll see project ideas for the Web in this section. These ideas for a project can be classified as tools of utility and education.

Here are the ideas behind the project:

- Content Aggregator
- Post -It Note
- Quiz Application
- URL Shortcutter
- Regex Request Device

## Aggregating Content

Content is gold. From blogs to social media platforms, it exists everywhere on the web. To keep up, you need to continuously check the Internet for new information. One way of staying updated is to manually check all of the sites to see what the new posts are. But it's time-consuming, and it's quite tiring.

This is where the aggregator of content comes in: A aggregator of content collects information from different places online and collects all of that information in one place. So, to get the latest information, you don't have to visit multiple sites: one site is enough.

With the content aggregator, you can get all the latest information from one site which aggregates all the content.

Examples of Content Aggregators

Here are some ideas for the Content Aggregator implementations:

- Hvper
- AllTop

## Application Info

The main goal of this idea for a project is to aggregate content. Next, you need to know from which places you 're going to use the web aggregator to get web. You can then use libraries such as requests to submit HTTP requests and BeautifulSoup to decode and scrape the content from the pages that are required.

As a background process, your application can implement its content aggregation. Therefore, libraries like ap-scheduler or celery can help. You can have an ap-scheduler try. It is great for small processes in the background.

You'll need to save it somewhere after you scrap content from different sites. So, you will use a database to save the content that has been scrapped.

## Extra Challenge

You can add more websites to an even harder challenge. This will help you learn how websites research and extract knowledge.

You can also have users subscribing to certain sites you are aggregate. The content aggregator will then, at the end of the day, send the articles for that day to the user's email address.

## Regex Call Tool

You and I handle text daily. There is a structure to this book, which is also text. This makes understanding easier for you. Sometimes, you need to find some information in text, and it may be ineffective to use the regular search tool in text editors.

It's here where the Regex Query Tool comes in. A regex is a collection of strings which means that the regex query tool can test the validity of the queries. Once the regex matches patterns in the text, this tells the user and highlights the patterns that match. Your Regex

Query Tool will check the user's passed in regex strings for validity.

Users can easily check the validity of their regex strings over the web with the Regex Query Tool. This makes it easier for them, rather than having to use a text editor to check the strings.

For instance, Regex Query Tools

Here are several Regex Query Device Implementations:

- RegexTester
- FreeFormatter

## Application Info

The main aim of this type of project is to tell the user the validity of the query strings that are entered. You can make it give a negative or positive response like Query String Is True and Query String Is Invalid, which implements the positive answer in green and the negative in red.

The query method doesn't need to be built from scratch. You can use the standard re library of Python, which you can use to run the query strings on the text you are entering. When the query string matches nothing, the re library returns None, and it returns the matched strings if positive.

Some users may not fully understand regex, so you can do a page explaining how regex works. You can create documentation that is sufficiently interesting to keep users excited about learning and understanding regex.

## Extra Challenge

It's fine to do a project that just returns the regex validity. But you can add a replacement function, too. This means that the application checks for regex validity and also allows users to replace the matched strings with something else. So, the tool is no longer a tool for finding but also a tool for replacing.

## URL Cutter

URLs can be incredibly long, and not easy to use. It's difficult when people share links or even try to remember a URL, because most URLs are filled with difficult characters and don't make meaningful words.

Here's where the Shortener URL comes in. A URL Shortener decreases the characters or letters in a URL and makes it easier to read and remember. A URL close to xyz.com/wwryb78&svnhkn%sghq? Sfiyh may be shortened to xyz.com/piojwr.

URLs are a joy to deal around with the URL Shortener.

For example, URL Shorteners

Here are some URL Shortener Implementations:

- Bitter
- MeShort

## Tech Details

This project idea's main aim is to shorten the URLs. The main task the application will perform is to shorten URLs, and then redirect users to the original URL when visiting the shortened URL.

The users input the original URL in the application, and the result will be the new, shortened URL. To do so, a blend of random and string modules can be used to generate the characters for the shortened URL.

You will need to save the original and shortened URLs in a database as users visit the shortened URL days, months, or years later. When a request enters, the application checks whether the URL exists and redirects to the original, or redirects it to a 404 page.

## Extra Challenge

Creating a shortened URL with random characters makes them shorter, random URLs better than the long ones. But you can make the users' outcome better. To customize URLs, you can add a feature, so users can customize the created URLs themselves.

Unquestionably, a custom xyz.com/mysite URL is

better than a randomly produced xyz.com/piojwr URL.

## Post-Remark

Having many thoughts and ideas in a day is normal but forgetting is also normal. One way of working around missing things is to pin them down before they disappear into thin air. Although some of the thoughts and ideas that were forgotten may be insignificant, some may be very important.

That is where a Post-It note comes in: A Post-It note is a small paper with low-tack adhesive on the back, making it fixable to surfaces such as papers, walls. Post-it notes make things easier to pin down. The idea for the Post-It Note project is something similar. It enables users to pinpoint things down, making them accessible anywhere, as it is a web application.

With the Post-It note, people can now track items everywhere, without the fear of missing stuff or misplacing notes — which is difficult for paper notes.

Post-it Notes for examples

Here are some Post-It Note Implementations:

- Note.ly
- Pinup

## Tech Details

This project's main objective is to allow users to track thoughts. This implies that each user will have their notes, so they will need to have an account creation feature in the application. This ensures every user's notes remain private to them.

Django comes with an authentication system for users, so it might be a good choice. You can use other frameworks such as a bottle or flask but the user authentication system will have to be implemented on your own.

Since users will need to classify their notes under different parts, the application would be more useful if a function is introduced to allow users to categorize their notes.

You may need notes on algorithms and data structures as an example, so you'll need to be able to distinguish the notes in those categories.

You may need to store every user's details and notes so that a database is an integral part of this project. The MySQLdb module can be used for a PostgreSQL database if you wish to use a MySQL database or a psycopg2 module. You can use other modules but it all depends on the database you choose to use.

## Extra Challenge

Since users are human in forgetting their ideas, it is also human for them to forget that they even made a note somewhere. You can add the functionality to remind users of their notes. This feature allows users to set a notification time and the application can send the alert by email to the users when it's time.

## Quiz Application

Know-how is strength. There are so many things to learn in the world, and quizzes help to test the understanding of those concepts. You do not have to understand everything about the language, as an intermediate Python developer. One way to figure out things you don't fully understand is to take tests.

That is where the question for a Quiz comes in. The Quiz Program will be asking users questions and requesting the correct answers to those questions. Think of the application of the Quiz as some kind of questionnaire.

Special users can call administrators will be allowed to create tests with the Quiz Application, so regular users can test their understanding and answer the questions of the subjects in the quiz.

## Types of Quiz requests

Here are a few implementations of the concept for the Quiz Application:

- myQuiz
- Kahoot

## Application Info

This project's main aim is to set quizzes and get people to answer them. Users should, therefore, be able to put questions and other users should be able to answer those questions. Afterward, the application will show the final score and the correct answers.

If you want users to be able to record their ratings, you may need to incorporate an account creation feature.

Users creating the tests should be able to create tests by simply uploading a text file with the questions and answers. The text file will have a format to choose from, so that the application can convert from a file to a quiz.

To do this project you will need to implement a database. For each user, the database will store the questions, potential answers, correct answers, and the scores.

## Extra Challenge

You can allow the users to add timers to the quizzes for more of a challenge. In this way, quiz developers will decide how many seconds or minutes a user will spend in the quiz on any question.

Having a quiz-sharing feature will be awesome too, so users can post fun quizzes with their friends on other platforms.

## Ideas for GUI project

You will see project ideas for Graphical User Interfaces in this section. These ideas for a project can be classified as tools for entertainment, finance, and utility.

Here are the ideas behind the project:

- MP3 Player
- Alarm Tool
- Film Administrator
- Expenditures Tracker

## MP3 Player

Audio is as important as, if not more important than, text today. Since audio files are digital files, you will need a playable tool to play them. You will never be able to listen to the content of an audio file without a player.

This is where the Player for MP3 enters. The MP3 Player is a computer where MP3s and other digital audio files are playable. This idea for a project MP3 Player GUI is trying to emulate the physical MP3 Player. You can create applications that let you play MP3 files on your laptop or desktop.

Upon construction of the MP3 Player project, users can play their MP3 files and other digital audio files without having to buy a physical MP3 Player. They'll be able to use their computers to play the MP3 files.

## MP3 Player Tests

Here are some MP3 Player Implementations:

The MusicBee

Foobar2000

Tech Details

This project's main aim is to allow users to play both digital audio files and MP3. The application needs to have a simple but beautiful user interface to be engaging to users.

You can have an interface with which to list the available MP3 files. You can also give users the option of listing other, non-MP3 digital audio files.

The users will also expect the MP3 Player to have an interface which will display information about the file being played. Some of the information that you can include are in minutes and seconds the file name, its length, the amount not played and the amount played.

Python has libraries that can play audio files in a few lines of code, such as Pygame, which enables you to work with multimedia files. You can also check out Simple Audio and Pymedia.

Many digital audio files can be handled by these libraries. They can handle certain types of files, not just those of MP3 files.

You can also introduce a feature that allows users to build a playlist. To do this, you will need a database to store information on the playlists that were made. The sqlite3 module from Python lets you use the SQLite database.

In this case, the SQLite database is a better option, since it is more file-based and simple to set up than other SQL databases. While SQLite is file-based, data conservation is better than a regular file.

## Extra Challenge

You may add a function to allow the MP3 player to repeat current playing files, or shuffle the list of files to be played, for a more exciting challenge.

A function that allows users to increase and decrease the play speed of the audio file may also be introduced.

This will be useful to users because they will be able to play files at a faster or slower speed than normal.

## Tool to alarm

As they say, "Tide and time wait for no man." But with so many things happening in our lives, it's hard not to lose track of time. A recall is required to be able to keep track of the time.

This is where the Alarm Tool comes in. An alarm is a device giving an audio or visual signal about a particular condition. This idea for the project Alarm Tool is an attempt to create an alarm as software. When a certain condition is met, the Alarm Tool gives an audio signal. In this case, the set time is the stated state.

With the Alarm Tool, users may set alarms at certain times of the day to remind them of things. The project Alarm Tool can operate from the user's laptop or desktop computer, so they don't have to buy a physical timer.

## Alarm Tools examples

Here are several Security Device Implementations:

- TimerForMac

- FreeAlarmClock

## Tech Details

This project's main objective is to trigger the audio signals at certain times of the day. So, the most important parts of the Alarm Tool are timing and the audio signal to be played.

The Alarm Tool should allow alarm formation, editing, and deletion by users. It should also have an interface that lists all the alarms, if the user has not deleted them. So, it will mention alarms that are active and inactive.

The application must play tones at the set time, since it is an alarm. There are audio-playing libraries, such as the Pygame library.

The application has to continue checking for set alarm times in your code logic. When the time is reached, the playing of the alarm tone activates a feature.

As the application must search for fixed alarm times, this means that the application will save the alarms in a database. The database will store such items as date, time, and location of the alarm.

## Extra Challenge

You can also allow users to set recurring alarms as an extra feature. They will be able to set alarms on certain days of the week, each week, that will ring at some time. For instance, an alarm can be set every Monday at 2:00 PM.

You can add a snooze feature, so your users can snooze alarms rather than just dismiss them.


## File Manager

The number of files on an average PC user's personal computer is fairly high. If all of those files are placed in a single directory, navigating and finding files or directories would be difficult. So, the files need to be arranged and managed correctly.

This is where a director of files comes in. A file manager allows users to access files and folders through a user interface. While files can be controlled via the command-line, not all users know how to do that.

Users can arrange, access, and manage their files and directories properly with a file manager, without knowing how to use the command line. Some of the tasks that a file manager does include copying, moving, and renaming files or directories.

## Examples of Tools in File Manager

Here are some ideas for the File Manager implementations:

- FreeCommander
- Explorer+++

## Tech Details

The file manager project's main objective is to provide the users with an interface to manage their files. Users want a file manager with a good looking and easy to use file management tool.

You can use the PySimpleGUI library without having to deal with a lot of complexity to create unique user interfaces with a powerful widget.

Your users should perform simple tasks such as creating new directories or emptying text files. They should also be able to copy directories or files, and move them.

For this project, the sys, os, and Shutil libraries will be very useful, because they can be used to perform actions on the context files while the user clicks away.

Today, grid views and list views are common views, so you can implement both in the app. This gives the user the option to select which view option fits them.

## Extra Challenge

To make the file manager somewhat more advanced, a search function can be implemented. In this way, users can search for files and directories without having to manually find them.

Also, you can implement a sorting feature. This will allow users to sort files by order, such as time, alphabetical order, or size.

## Expenditure Tracker

We have daily expenses ranging from foodstuffs to clothing to bills. There are so many expenses that it is normal to lose track of them and continue to spend until we are nearly out of cash. A tracker will help people look out for their expenses.

It's here that the expense tracker comes in. An expense tracker is a software tool enabling users to keep track of their spending. Depending on how advanced it is, it can also analyze the expenses, but let's keep it simple for now.

Users can set a budget with the expense tracker and track their expenditures so they can make better financial decisions.

## Examples of Tracker Expenses

Here are some of the Cost Tracker Concept implementations:

- Gnucash
- Buddi

## Tech Details

This project's main aim is to keep track of user expenses. Some statistical analysis must be done to allow users to get accurate information about their expenditures and to help them spend better.

While monitoring the expenses is crucial, it is also necessary to have a good GUI. You can create a unique interface with PySimpleGUI to improve the user's experience.

PyData libraries like matplotlib and pandas can help to create an expense tracker.

The pandas' library can be used in the analysis of data, and the matplotlib library can be used for graph plotting. Graphs will provide the users with a visual representation of their expenses and usually, a visual representation is easier to understand.

The application will get users data. The data here are the expenses inputted. So, the expenses will have to be stored in a database. For this project, the SQLite database is a good database option because it can be set up easily. The SQLite database can be used with the sqlite3 module.

## Extra Challenge

For your users to benefit from this project, they will have to periodically enter their expenses which will slip their minds. Implementing a notification feature might be helpful for you. So, at certain times of the day or the week, the application will send a notification, reminding them to use the expense tracker.

## Ideas for a command-line project

In this section, you will see command-line project ideas. The ideas discussed for the project can be classified as utility tools.

Here are the ideas behind the project:

- Contact Book
- File Connectivity Checker
- Bulk File Rename Tool
- Directory Tree Generator

## Contact library

We come across a lot of people every day. We make friends and acquaintances. We are getting their contacts to keep in contact later. Sadly, keeping the contact details you have received can be difficult. One way to achieve this is to write down the contact details. But this is not secure as you can easily lose the physical book.

Here's where the project Contact Book comes in. A contact book is a tool to save details about a contact, such as name, telephone number, address, and email address. For this project contact sheet, you can create a software tool that lets people save and find contact information.

Users can save their contacts with the concept of the contact book project, with less chance of losing the saved contact information. It will always be accessible through the command-line from their computer.

## Examples of Software for Contacts

There are Contact Book applications, but finding Contact Book products on the command line is rare, as most are Mobile, Web, or GUI applications.

Below are some Contact Book Implementations:

- Pobuca Connect
- Simple Contacts

## Tech Details

This project's main purpose is to save the contact information. Set up the users' commands for entering contact details. You can use the argparse, or click frameworks on the command line. They abstract a lot of complicated things, so when executing commands, you just have to concentrate on the logic to be run.

Some of the features that you should implement include the contact deletion commands, listing saved contacts, and updating contact information. You may also allow users to list contacts using different criteria, such as alphabetic order or date of contact formation.

The SQLite database will be fine for saving contacts as it is a command-line project. SQLite is an easy-to-use setup. You can save the contact information in a file, but a file doesn't provide the advantages you can get from using SQLite, such as performance and protection.

The Python sqlite3 module will be very useful in using the SQLite database in this project.

## Extra Challenge

Remember how do you store the database on your computer? What if something, like the user losing their files, happens? It means that they will lose the contact information, too.

You can also push yourself and transfer your account to an online storage site. To do so, at some times you can upload database files to the cloud.

Also, you can add a command allowing users to backup the database themselves. This way, if the database file is lost the user can still have access to the contacts.

You should remember that some form of identification may be needed, so that the contact book can say which database file belongs to which user. Implementing an authentication function for users is one way to get things done.

## Site Connectivity Checker

When you visit a URL, you expect your browser to view the requested links. But not always this is the case. Sometimes the sites may be down, so that you won't get the results you want. Instead, error notices will be sent to you. You can continue to try a down site until it arrives and you get the information you need.

This is where the project joins the Site Connection Checker. The Site Connectivity Checker visits a URL and returns the URL status: it may or may not be active. At intervals, the Site Connectivity Checker will visit the URL, returning the results of each session.

Instead of visiting a URL manually, a Site Connectivity Checker will do all the manual work for you. So, you'll just get the results of the search without having to

waste time on the browser, waiting for the site to go live.

## Site Connectivity Checker Examples

Here are some of the Site Connection Checker implementation ideas:

- Site24x7
- Ping

## Application Info

This project's main objective is to check the status of the sites. So, to test a website's status, you must write code.

You may choose either to use TCP or ICMP for your connections. One for checking out is the socket module. Socket Programming can also be read in Python (Guide).

You can attach commands to allow users to add and remove sites from the list of sites to be reviewed through your chosen system, be it the button, Docopt, or Argparse frame.

Also, users should be able to start the tool, stop it and determine the intervals.

Since the list of files to be checked will have to be saved, you can either use an SQLite database through the sqlite3 module or save it in a file (just a list of sites).

## Extra Challenge

The application will monitor the site's connection status and show the results to the command-line. But that will allow the user to keep the command-line verified.

You will raise the difficulty and get a notification feature implemented. The notification feature may be a sound that is played in the background to alert the user when a site changes its status. To store a site's prior status, you'll need a database. That is the only way the tool can tell about change of status.

## Bulk File Rename Tool

Sometimes, all the files in a directory must be named according to certain conventions. For example, in a directory with File0001.jpg, you can name all the files, where the numbers are increasing based on the number of files in the directory. That can be stressful and repetitive to do manually.

The Bulk File Rename Tool enable users to rename a large number of files, without the need to rename files manually.

That saves a lot of time for the users. It saves them the trouble of having to do routine, boring work, and making mistakes. Users can rename files in a few seconds with the Bulk File Rename Tool, without any mistakes.

## Examples of Tools to Rename Bulk Files

Here are several implementations of the concept of renaming Bulk File:

- Rename
- Ren

## Application Info

The main goal of this idea for a project is to rename files. Therefore, the application has to find a way to manipulate the target files. The libraries os, sys, and shutil will be useful for much of this project.

Using naming conventions your users will be able to rename all the files in the directory. They should, therefore, be able to pass choice in the naming convention. If you understand how regex functions, the regex module can help suit the appropriate naming patterns.

A user may want to pass as part of the commands in a naming convention like my files, and expect the tool to rename all the files like myfilesXYZ, where XYZ is a number. Also, they should be able to select the directory where the files to be renamed are.

## Extra Challenge

The big challenge in this project is renaming all of the files in a directory. However, users may need to name just a specific number of files. To test your skills, you can implement a feature that allows users to select the number of files to be renamed, rather than all the files.

Note that renaming only several files allows the application to arrange the files based on alphabetical order, file size, or file creation time, depending on the user 's needs.

## Tree Directory Generator

Directories are similar to family trees: each directory has a special relationship to other directories. No directories, except an empty root directory, ever remain on its own.

It is difficult to see the connection between folders when you're dealing with files and directories, because you can only see what's in the current directory. You use a file manager, or you work from the command line.

You can see the relation between files and directories like a tree or map with a Directory Tree Generator.

This makes the positioning of the files and directories easier to understand. When explaining certain concepts, a directory treemap is important, and a generator of directory tree

makes it easier to obtain a visual representation of the relationships between files and directories.

## Examples of Tree Generators in Directories

Here are some Directory Tree Generator Implementations:

- Dirtreex
- Tree

## Application Info

The Directory Tree Generator's main objective is to visualize the connections between files and directories. The os library can be very useful to list the files and directories in a selected directory.

Using a framework like Argparse or Docopt helps to abstract loads of things, allowing you to concentrate on writing code for the logic of the application.

In the logic of the application, you can decide how files or directories you want to represent. It's a brilliant way to go about it using different colors. The colored library can be used to print files and folders in various colors.

Also, you can determine how far you want the Directory Tree Generator to go. For instance, if a directory has children directories twelve deep levels, you may only decide to go as deep as the fifth level.

You can also let the user decide how deeply they want the Directory Tree Generator to go, if you wish.

## Extra Challenge

Since the results will be on the command-line of the generated directory tree, you can go one step further. You can have the generator create directory tree images so it will essentially turn the text into an image.

The pillow library would be useful for doing this.

## Tips to Project Works

It can be tough working on projects. That's one reason why project motivation and interest will make it a less daunting task.

If you're interested in a project, you 're going to be able to spend time researching as well as finding libraries and tools to help with the project.

**Here are a few hints:**

- Consider motivational sources
- Bridge the project to subtasks
- Do some subtask research
- Make every subtask, one step at a time
- Get help in case you 're stuck
- Put up the subtasks

# CONCLUSION

Now that you've learned the basics of Python, you're ready to try your hand at simple but very satisfying projects.

Because that's the beauty of Python: even with the basics, which you assimilate in a short time, you can create exciting programs and projects.

My advice, however, is to go back to the beginning of the book and reread everything once again, so you can make your own the basic concepts of this programming language.

Python, in fact, is one of the most popular and important programming languages. Mastering it the right way can help you work your way up the corporate ladder, enrich your analytical skills, and simply put, it can provide you with new and exciting challenges every day and hours of fun.

If, however, you feel you need more and are ready to deepen your knowledge, I recommend you check out the other volumes in the series:

- **BASIC PYTHON COMMANDS**
- **ADVANCED PYTHON COMMANDS**

- **PYTHON PRACTICAL APPLICATIONS and**
- **PYTHON TUTORIALS.**